A Barrel of
GOOD CLEAN
Jokes
FOR KIDS

BOB PHILLIPS

HARVEST HOUSE PUBLISHERS
EUGENE, OREGON

Cover design by Dugan Design Group

Cover photo © rost9 / fotolia

HARVEST KIDS is a trademark of The Hawkins Children's LLC. Harvest House Publishers, Inc., is the exclusive licensee of the trademark HARVEST KIDS.

A Barrel of Good Clean Jokes for Kids
Published by Harvest House Publishers
Eugene, Oregon 97408
www.harvesthousepublishers.com

Some material previously published in…
  Extremely Good Clean Jokes for Kids
  Good Clean Jokes to Drive Your Parents Crazy
  All-Time Awesome Collection of Good Clean Jokes
  The Best of the Good Clean Jokes

ISBN 978-0-7369-7888-0 (pbk.)
ISBN 978-0-7369-7889-7 (eBook)

Printed in the United States of America

20 21 22 23 24 25 26 27 28 / BP-GL / 10 9 8 7 6 5 4 3 2 1

Contents

1

Little-Known Facts About Animals

Q: What do you do with a seasick rhinoceros?

A: You get out of the way.

* * *

Q: What is black and white and slowly turning blue?

A: A zebra in the Arctic.

* * *

Q: What does a polar bear wear when his head is cold?

A: An ice cap.

* * *

Q: What underwater predator buys all your valuables?

A: A loan shark.

* * *

Q: What does a whale call a bunch of fish swimming together?

A: A school lunch.

* * *

Q: What is a rabbit's favorite kind of exercise?

A: Hareobics.

* * *

Q: What has antlers and likes to be outside when it's wet?

A: A rain deer.

* * *

Q: How much are a dozen skunks worth?

A: Twelve scents.

* * *

Q: How much money is a herd of deer worth?

A: It depends on how many bucks are in it.

* * *

Q: How do you stop rabbits from eating up your garden?

A: Spray them with hare remover.

* * *

Q: How do skunks talk to each other?

A: On their smell phones.

* * *

Q: How do spiders make phone calls?

A: With crawler ID.

* * *

Q: How do cheetahs make phone calls?

A: With speed dial.

* * *

Q: What do frogs like to sit on?

A: Toadstools.

* * *

Q: How did the turtle pay for his ice cream cone?

A: He shelled out cash.

* * *

Q: How do you get dragon milk?

A: From a cow with short legs.

* * *

Q: What sea mammal is very famous?

A: The presidential seal.

* * *

Q: Which came first, the chicken or the egg?

A: The chicken. God wouldn't lay an egg.

* * *

Q: How do you stop a frog from dying?

A: Help him to stop croaking.

* * *

Q: What kind of bread do rabbits eat?

A: Hole wheat.

* * *

Q: What did Mrs. Coyote say to the baby coyote when she put him to bed?

A: Pheasant dreams.

* * *

Q: What did one porcupine say to another?

A: Quit needling me!

* * *

Q: What is a kangaroo's favorite game?

A: Hopscotch.

* * *

Q: What do rabbits like to eat for dessert?

A: Carrot cake.

* * *

Q: What happened to the frog when he didn't put money into the parking meter?

A: He got toad away.

* * *

Q: What do skunks take with them when they go to war?

A: Stink bombs.

* * *

Q: What kind of stories do rabbits tell?

A: Cotton tales.

* * *

Q: How do you catch a bunny rabbit?

A: With a hare net.

* * *

Q: What has eleven ears and a cotton tail?

A: A rabbit sitting on a pile of corn.

* * *

Q: How did one mouse revive another mouse?

A: With mouse-to-mouse resuscitation.

* * *

Q: What did the bear say to the lion?

A: You look beastly.

* * *

Q: What did one boa constrictor say to the other?

A: I have a crush on you.

* * *

Q: What animal tells tall tales?

A: The giraffe.

* * *

Q: What is a squirrel's favorite flower?

A: Forget-me-nuts.

* * *

Q: How does a bison pay for his dinner?

A: With a buffalo bill.

* * *

Q: What is a lion's territory called?

A: The mane land.

* * *

Q: What does a gorilla wear when he barbecues?

A: An ape-ron.

* * *

Q: Which jungle animal is always complaining?

A: A whine-oceros.

* * *

Q: What newspaper do seals like to read?

A: The *Walrus Street Journal*.

* * *

Q: What does a boa constrictor say when it bumps into people?

A: Exqueeze me.

* * *

Q: What kind of cat likes to go surfing?

A: A sea lion.

* * *

Q: What kind of fish never tells the truth?

A: Abaloney.

* * *

Q: What animals have tunnel vision?

A: Moles and gophers.

* * *

Q: What do baby snakes like to play with?

A: Their rattles.

* * *

Q: Which animals can jump higher than the Statue of Liberty?

A: All the animals can. The Statue of Liberty can't jump.

* * *

Q: What did all the jungle animals say to the lawyer?

A: "So zoo us."

* * *

Q: What does a fish sleep on?

A: A waterbed.

* * *

Q: What track event is popular in the arctic?

A: The polar vault.

* * *

Q: How do you stop a skunk from smelling?

A: Put a clothespin on its nose.

* * *

Q: What did the boy turtle say to the girl turtle?

A: Shell we go for a walk?

* * *

Q: What do you say to a giraffe who is feeling sad?

A: Keep your chin up.

* * *

Q: How do you stop mice from squeaking?

A: Use an oil can.

* * *

Q: Where do fish sleep?

A: In riverbeds.

* * *

Q: What type of stool does an octopus need?

A: A foot, foot, foot, foot, foot, foot, foot, foot stool.

* * *

Q: What did the older ape say to the younger ape?

A: You're a chimp off the ol' block.

* * *

Q: What do alligators use to cook in?

A: A crockpot.

* * *

Q: What animal is always on pins and needles?

A: A porcupine.

* * *

Q: What did one kangaroo say to the other kangaroo?

A: I hop you have a nice day.

* * *

Q: What do you use to tie up a pig?

A: A hamstring.

* * *

Q: How do cows get to school?

A: They ride in moooving vans.

* * *

Q: How do squids travel in the ocean?

A: On an octobus.

* * *

Q: How do rabbits like to travel?

A: On a hare plane.

* * *

Q: How do you catch a school of fish?

A: You use bookworms.

* * *

Q: Where do cows submit their short stories?

A: In the school moosepaper.

* * *

Q: What two animals do you take to bed?

A: Two calves.

* * *

Q: Where does a sheep get its hair cut?

A: At the baa-baa shop.

* * *

Q: Which eats more grass, black sheep or white sheep?

A: White sheep because there are more of them.

* * *

Q: What does a pig use when he makes notes at school?

A: A pigpen.

* * *

Q: What do you call a race for furry woodland animals?

A: A foxtrot.

* * *

Q: What's a lion's favorite song lyric?

A: "Roar, roar, roar your boat gently down the stream…"

* * *

Q: How do you know when a lion is happy?

A: It roars with laughter.

* * *

Q: How does a rhinoceros cross a busy road?

A: He uses his horn.

* * *

Q: What do penguins ride at amusement parks?

A: Polar coasters.

* * *

Q: What did the frog say when he ordered a hamburger?

A: Can I have flies with that?

* * *

Q: What is a cat's favorite color?

A: Purrrrple.

* * *

Q: What is a chick's favorite drink?

A: Peepsi.

* * *

Q: Where do you send a sick pig?

A: To the hogspital.

* * *

Q: What kind of sandals do frogs wear?

A: Open toad.

* * *

Q: If a dog lost its tail, where would it get another one?

A: At the retail store.

* * *

Q: What do giraffes have that no other animals have?

A: Baby giraffes.

* * *

Q: What kind of fish do you find in a bird cage?

A: A perch.

* * *

Q: What is worse than a giraffe with a sore throat?

A: A centipede with blisters.

* * *

Q: What bird can lift the heaviest weight?

A: A crane.

* * *

Q: What goes tick, tock, woof?

A: A watchdog.

* * *

Q: What kinds of birds are kept in captivity more than any others?

A: Jailbirds.

* * *

Q: What animal is both small and large at the same time?

A: A jumbo shrimp.

* * *

Q: What kind of a bone should you not give to a dog?

A: A trombone.

* * *

Q: How does a pig get to the hospital?

A: In a hambulance.

* * *

Q: Where do cats like to go on vacation?

A: The Canary Islands.

* * *

Q: Where do tadpoles go to change into frogs?

A: The croakroom.

* * *

Q: What kind of bugs are good at math?

A: Arithmaticks.

* * *

Q: What's the best way to stop a rhinoceros from jumping up and down on the bed?

A: Put crazy glue on the ceiling.

* * *

Q: What does the government use when it takes a census of all the monkeys in the zoo?

A: An ape recorder.

* * *

Q: What kind of animal always is found at baseball games?

A: The bat.

* * *

Q: What happened when the duck was interrogated?

A: It quacked under pressure.

* * *

Q: What kind of bird eats the same worm eight times?

A: A swallow with the hiccups.

* * *

Q: What is the difference between a cat and a bullfrog?

A: The cat has nine lives, but the bullfrog croaks every night.

* * *

Q: What has four legs and flies?

A: A horse.

* * *

Q: What do you give pet mice with bad breath?

A: Mousewash.

* * *

Q: What's the difference between a cat and a hockey puck?

A: About two IQ points.

* * *

Q: How does a caterpillar make a new start?

A: He turns over a new leaf.

* * *

Q: What is the difference between a cat and a match?

A: The cat lights on its feet, and a match lights on its head.

Strange Breeds

Q: What do you get if you cross an Australian animal with a cheerleader?

A: A kangarooter.

* * *

Q: What do you get if you spill boiling water down the rabbit hole?

A: Hot, cross bunnies.

* * *

Q: What do you get if you cross an elephant with a vacuum?

A: Something that sucks up a lot of peanuts.

* * *

Q: What do you get if you cross a centipede with an elephant?

A: You get out of the way as fast as you can!

* * *

Q: What do you get if you cross a porcupine with a peacock?

A: A sharp dresser.

* * *

Q: What do you get when you cross a clock and a chicken?

A: An alarm cluck.

* * *

Q: What do you get when you cross a cow and a pogo stick?

A: A milkshake.

* * *

Q: What do you get when you cross a worm and a fur coat?

A: A caterpillar.

* * *

Q: What do you get if you cross a rattlesnake with a doughnut?

A: A reptile that rattles and rolls.

* * *

Q: What do you get when you cross a pony and a cockroach?

A: A horse and buggy.

* * *

Q: What would you get if you crossed a dog with a cartoon sailor?

A: Pupeye.

* * *

Q: What would you get if you crossed a prehistoric elephant with a flock of sheep?

A: A very woolly mammoth.

Insane Inventions

Q: What do you get when you cross a motorcycle with a joke book?

A: A yamahaha.

***

Q: What do you get when you cross a gangster and a garbage man?

A: Organized grime.

***

Q: What do you get when you cross an outdoor cinema and a swimming pool?

A: A dive-in theater.

***

Q: What do you get if you add 8,136 and 7,257, subtract 93, and divide the answer by 5?

A: A headache.

***

Q: What do you get when a surgeon removes a healthy appendix with a blunt scalpel?

A: A pointless operation.

A Long Day at School

Q: Why can't you take a giraffe to school?

A: It won't fit in your backpack.

***

Q: What do you say when the school lunch server gives you a hot dog?

A: Franks a lot.

***

Q: What happens to those who don't pass a social studies class?

A: History will repeat itself.

***

Q: What class gives extra credit for passing notes?

A: Music class.

***

Q: Why did the music student get low grades at school?
A: He kept getting into treble.

* * *

Q: What is the worst sport to play in school?
A: Bad-minton.

* * *

Q: What is a snake's favorite subject?
A: Ssscience.

* * *

Q: What is a snake's second-favorite subject?
A: Hissstory.

* * *

Q: In what class do students who act up get As?
A: Drama class.

* * *

Q: What color of books get the best grades?
A: The ones that are red.

* * *

Q: When did Frosty the Snowman start school?

A: In frost grade.

* * *

Q: What's the cat's favorite class at school?

A: Meowsic.

* * *

Q: How do bees, hornets, and wasps get to school?

A: They take the school buzz.

* * *

Q: What happened when the omelet acted up in school?

A: It got eggspelled.

* * *

Q: What is the most relaxing part of school?

A: De-tension.

* * *

Q: What activity did Jack Frost like best in school?

A: Snow and tell.

* * *

Q: Where can students get an A for cutting class?

A: In barber school.

* * *

Q: Why did the two science teachers get married?

A: Their chemistry was just right.

* * *

Q: What did the farmer like best in school?

A: Learning about square roots.

* * *

Q: What kind of books do you find in a Catholic girls' school?

A: Nunfiction.

* * *

Q: Why did the conductor do poorly in school?

A: He lost his train of thought.

* * *

Q: Why did the student with a cold get sent to the principal's office?

A: His nose kept running in the halls.

* * *

Q: Why was the watch sent to the principal's office?

A: It was always making faces.

* * *

Q: Why was the clock sent to the principal's office?

A: It tocked too much.

* * *

Q: Why was the egg sent to the principal's office?

A: It kept telling yolks in class.

* * *

Q: Why was the shoelace sent to the principal's office?

A: Because it was acting knotty.

* * *

Q: Where do they put naughty principals?

A: In the corner office.

* * *

Q: What does the high school basketball team practice at snack time?

A: Dunking donuts.

* * *

Q: Which students do best at the circus school?

A: The class clowns.

* * *

Q: What do you need to stay in medical school?

A: Lots of patients.

* * *

Q: What do you call a class about carbonation?

A: Fizz ed.

* * *

Q: How do gymnasts read a book quickly?

A: By flipping through the pages.

* * *

Q: What was the kangaroo's favorite part of the school year?

A: Spring break.

* * *

Q: What did the student give his mean teacher?

A: A crabapple.

* * *

Q: Why was the lizard chosen for the school baseball team?

A: He was good at catching flies.

* * *

Q: What was Sherlock Holmes's first school?

A: Elementary.

* * *

Q: Where do they send dishonest students?

A: To the liebrary.

* * *

Q: What class in school draws the most students?

A: The art class.

* * *

Q: What is a swimmer's favorite class?

A: Diver's ed.

* * *

Q: Where do bookkeepers spend their time in school?

A: In the audit-orium.

* * *

Q: What do you call someone who has a straight-A report card in their back pocket?

A: Smarty pants.

* * *

Q: What kind of books do students read in Dallas?

A: Tex books.

* * *

Q: Why did the boy swallow the dollar bill his mother gave him?

A: It was lunch money.

* * *

Q: Why did the teacher pass out masks and fins with the report cards?

A: Everyone's grades were under C level.

* * *

Q: How do cheerleaders talk to each other?

A: On their yell phones.

* * *

Q: Why are rabbits so good at math?

A: Because they multiply so quickly.

* * *

Q: What does the teacher send home with the pig?

A: Hamwork.

* * *

Q: What lunch is served to lazy students?

A: Meatloaf.

* * *

Q: What is a math teacher's favorite dessert?

A: Pumpkin pi.

* * *

Q: Did you hear the joke about the pencil?

A: It was pointless.

* * *

Q: What is the cheapest school snack?

A: Freetos.

* * *

Q: How do you know a hippopotamus is in your locker?

A: You can't shut the door.

* * *

Q: Why did the math teacher go to the counselor?

A: Because he had lots of problems.

* * *

Q: Who is the golf coach's favorite student?

A: The teacher's putt.

* * *

Q: What is the favorite bread for straight-A students?

A: The honor roll.

* * *

Q: What do temporary teachers eat for lunch?

A: Sub sandwiches.

* * *

Q: In what month of the year does the school band play the best music?

A: March.

* * *

Q: What do you call it when you get an A-plus on a test?

A: A surprise.

* * *

Q: What school do football quarterbacks go to?

A: Hike school.

* * *

Q: What grade did the chiropractic student get on his report card?

A: Straight aches.

* * *

Q: Why did the students fail drivers ed?

A: They took a crash course.

* * *

Q: Where do monsters go to college?

A: Gooniversities.

* * *

Q: How do college students from the other side of the lake get to school?

A: They take scholarships.

* * *

Q: What tests do students take to graduate from dental school?

A: Oral exams.

* * *

Q: What do you call someone who's good at geometry and sports?

A: A mathlete.

* * *

Q: What happened when the jump rope did well in school?

A: It skipped a grade.

* * *

Q: Why was the student disappointed with his computer class?

A: He was key-bored.

* * *

Q: Why is going to school like taking a bath?

A: After you're in it a while, it's not so hot.

* * *

Boy: I think I have the measles.

School counselor: That's a rash statement.

* * *

Boy: When I grow up, I want to own an ice cream shop.

School counselor: I think you should go to sundae school.

* * *

First girl: Why did you get kicked out of drivers ed?

Second girl: It was an accident.

* * *

Boy: I keep seeing imaginary sheep.

School counselor: That's baaaaad.

* * *

Boy: I want to be a soccer player when I grow up.

School counselor: I think you'll have a ball.

* * *

First boy: I'm going to try out for the school hockey team.

Second boy: Good puck.

* * *

The teacher says that I need to learn all about decimals.
    But I just don't get the point.

* * *

Boy: Help me—I think I'm invisible.

School counselor: I'm sorry, I can't see you right now.

* * *

Teacher: Where is Nevada?

Student: I don't have the Vegas idea.

* * *

Teacher: If you had three pop tarts in your lunch and one of your friends asked for one, how many pop tarts would you have left?

Student: Three.

* * *

First boy: I'm taking an astronomy class.

Second boy: I guess you'll just be taking up space.

* * *

Student: I think I'm a deck of cards.

School counselor: Just deal with it!

* * *

Teacher: What body of water do you find between the Atlantic and the Pacific oceans?

Student: Tennes-sea.

* * *

Student: Nobody takes me seriously.

Counselor: Ha, ha, ha!

* * *

Teacher: What was the Gettysburg address?

Student: The place where the Gettysburgs lived.

* * *

Teacher: What is your favorite aquatic sport?

Student: Channel surfing.

* * *

Parent: Are you doing good in Spanish class?

Student: *Si.*

Parent: Oh well, we can't all be A students.

* * *

First student: Why did you drop out of medical school?

Second student: I was sick of doing all the homework.

* * *

Parent: How did you like your study about sponges?

Student: I couldn't absorb all the information.

* * *

First student: What are you reading?

Second student: A mystery.

First student: But that's an algebra textbook, isn't it?

Second student: Yep.

* * *

Teacher: How many days of the week end in Y?

Student: Nine—Monday, Tuesday, Wednesday, Thursday, Friday, Saturday, Sunday, today, and yesterday!

* * *

Teacher: What is the name of the man who discovered gravity?

Student: I've been wondering the same thing myself.

* * *

Boy: Guess what, Mom? I got a 100 in school today.

Mother: That's great!

Boy: Yeah, I got 20 in math, 37 in science, 23 in English, and 20 in reading.

* * *

First boy: I failed every subject but Spanish.

Second boy: How did you do that?

First boy: I didn't take Spanish.

* * *

Boy: My teacher yelled at me for something I didn't do!

Mother: That doesn't sound fair. What was it?

Boy: My homework.

* * *

Teacher: Sally, I was just reading over this letter you did. Your inputting is really improving. I see there are only seven mistakes here.

Student: Thank you!

Teacher: Now let's take a look at the second line.

* * *

Teacher: Does anyone have a garbage disposal at home?

Student: Yes, ma'am, we have one, but it isn't in the house.

Teacher: Then where is it?

Student: Out in the pigpen.

* * *

Teacher: Tell me about the Iron Age.

Student: Sorry, I'm a little rusty on that subject.

* * *

Teacher: If I had ten oranges in one hand and six in the other, what would I have?

Student: Big hands.

* * *

Teacher: A job well done need not be done again.

Student: What about mowing the lawn?

* * *

Teacher: If you insist on talking, I'll have to send you to the principal's office.

Student: Oh, does the principal need somebody to talk to?

✳ ✳ ✳

A letter sent home by a teacher: "Lester is trying—very."

✳ ✳ ✳

Teacher: Name four animals that belong to the cat family.

Student: The mama cat, the papa cat, and two kittens.

✳ ✳ ✳

Teacher: Did you reprimand your little boy for mimicking me?

Parent: Yes, I told him not to act like a fool.

✳ ✳ ✳

Teacher: Birds, though small, are remarkable creatures. For example, what can a bird do that I can't do?

Student: Take a bath in a saucer.

✳ ✳ ✳

Teacher: This is the fifth day this week you're late! What do you have to say for yourself?

Student: I'm sure glad it's Friday.

✳ ✳ ✳

Teacher: How would you treat a pig that's been stung by a bee?

Student: Apply oinkment.

* * *

Mother: Are there any unusual children in your class?

Boy: Yes, three of them have good manners.

* * *

Mother: Are you acting responsibly at school?

Boy: Absolutely. Every time something goes wrong at school, my teacher says I'm responsible.

* * *

Teacher: There will be only a half day of school this morning.

Students: Whoopee! Hooray!

Teacher: We'll have the other half this afternoon.

5

Waiter, Waiter...

Customer: Waiter, there's a footprint on my scrambled eggs!

Waiter: Yes, sir. You ordered an omelet and told me to step on it.

* * *

Customer: Waiter, there's no chicken in my chicken soup!

Waiter: There is no horse in horseradish, either.

* * *

Customer: Waiter, why is your finger on my steak?

Waiter: To keep it from falling on the floor again.

* * *

Customer: Waiter, there's a fly in my soup!

Waiter: Don't worry, sir. The spider on the bread will take care of it.

* * *

Customer: Is your water supply healthy?

Waiter: Yes, sir. We only use well water.

* * *

Customer: Waiter, I'm so hungry I could eat a horse!

Waiter: You came to the right place.

* * *

Customer: You brought me the wrong order.

Waiter: Yes, sir. You said you wanted something different.

* * *

Customer: This coffee tastes like mud.

Waiter: Well, it was ground this morning.

* * *

Customer: I'm in a hurry. Will the hot cakes be long?

Waiter: No, they're round.

* * *

Customer: Is it customary to tip the waiter in this restaurant?

Waiter: Yes, sir.

Customer: Then hand me a tip. I've waited almost an hour for my steak.

Name That Animal

Q: What do you call a cat with eight legs?

A: An octo-pus.

***

Q: What do you call a ram that lives at the top of a mountain?

A: A hillbilly goat.

***

Q: What do you call a rabbit with a broken leg?

A: Unhoppy.

***

Q: What do you call a warrior rodent?

A: Chinchilla the Hun.

***

Q: What do you call a big, well-dressed cat?

A: A dandy lion.

***

Q: What do you call nice guys who smell like skunks?

A: A phew good men.

* * *

Q: What do you call a grizzly without any fur?

A: Bear naked.

* * *

Q: What do you call a bunny that rides racehorses?

A: A jock rabbit.

* * *

Q: What do you call a squirrel with a hammer?

A: A nutcracker.

* * *

Q: What do you call a cow without any legs?

A: Ground beef.

* * *

Q: What do you call a young cat's trash?

A: Kitty litter.

* * *

Q: What do you call a talkative ox?

A: A yakety yak.

* * *

Q: What do you call a monkey who always tells the truth?

A: Honest Ape.

* * *

Q: What do you call a camel without a hump?

A: Humpfree.

* * *

Q: What do you call a monkey who gossips all the time?

A: A blaboon.

* * *

Q: What do you call a kangaroo who goes to the Olympics?

A: A jumping jock.

* * *

Q: What do you call a pig that has been healed?

A: Cured ham.

* * *

Q: What do you call a health drink for rabbits?

A: Hare tonic.

* * *

Q: What do you call a smart-aleck duck?

A: A wise quacker.

* * *

Q: What do you call a pig driving a car?

A: A road hog.

* * *

Q: What do you call a chick with bad manners?

A: A mockingbird.

* * *

Q: What do you call an angry rabbit?

A: Hopping mad.

* * *

Q: What do you call a bee that talks in very low tones?

A: A mumblebee.

* * *

Q: What do you call a bug that arrests other bugs?

A: A coproach.

* * *

Q: What do you call a kangaroo that has no pep?

A: Out of bounds.

7

Whatchamacallit

Q: What do you call a book with a car as the main character?

A: An autobiography.

***

Q: Whom do you call a bad driver?

A: The guy you run into.

***

Q: What do you call someone who takes pom-poms to the garden?

A: A cheerweeder.

***

Q: What you call someone who takes pom-poms to the library?

A: A cheerreader.

***

Q: What do you call someone who waves pom-poms and insults people?

A: A jeerleader.

* * *

Q: What you call someone who waves pom-poms and is always crying?

A: A tearleader.

* * *

Q: What do you call someone who is always afraid and carries pom-poms?

A: A fearleader.

* * *

Q: What do you call a lump on a policeman's foot?

A: Corn on the cop.

* * *

Q: What do you call a math assignment for rabbits?

A: Hare problems.

* * *

Q: What do you call a bathtub for pigs?

A: Hogwash.

* * *

Q: What do you call a test about dogs?

A: A pup quiz.

* * *

Q: What do you call a quiz for prisoners?

A: A contest.

* * *

Q: What do you call a hot dog when it's in a bad mood?

A: A crankfurter.

* * *

Q: What do you call the man who cuts lions' hair?

A: The mane man.

8

Oddball Definitions

Acquaintance: a person you know well enough to borrow
money from but not well enough to lend money to

* * *

Alarm clock: a frightened timepiece

* * *

Amiss: someone who is not married

* * *

Amount: what a soldier in the cavalry rides

* * *

Appeal: what a banana comes in

* * *

Applause: two hands slapping each other's faces

* * *

Atoll: what you pay before you cross a bridge

* * *

Author: a guy who is usually write

* * *

Bank robber: a guy who gets alarmed easily

* * *

Beastly weather: raining cats and dogs

* * *

Bore: a person who insists on talking about himself when you want to talk about yourself

* * *

Boycott: a bed for a male child

* * *

College cheer: money from home

* * *

Carpet: a cat or dog who enjoys riding in an automobile

* * *

Coffee: break fluid

* * *

Complement: the applause that refreshes

* * *

Dandruff: chips off the old block

* * *

Duck: a chicken with snowshoes

* * *

Endangered species: a kid who gets straight Fs on his report card

* * *

Falsehood: someone who pretends to be a gangster

* * *

Finland: where sharks live

* * *

Fireproof: the boss's relatives

* * *

Flood: a river too big for its bridges

* * *

Flashlight: a case to carry dead batteries in

* * *

Flabbergasted: the state of being overwhelmed by flabber

* * *

Fodder: a man married to a mudder

* * *

Gruesome: a little taller than before

* * *

High heels: the invention of a girl who had been kissed on the forehead one too many times

* * *

Horse sense: stable thinking

* * *

Hypodermic needle: a stick-shooter

* * *

Knapsack: a sleeping bag

* * *

Laugh: a smile that burst

* * *

Little leaguer: peanut batter

* * *

Love: a heart attack

* * *

Overeating: an activity that will make you thick to your
stomach

* * *

Pedestrian: a father of kids who can drive

* * *

Screen door: what kids get a bang out of

* * *

Stationery store: a shop that stays pretty much at the same
location

* * *

Stork: the bird with a big bill

* * *

Stucco: what you get when you sit on gummo

* * *

Sweater: a garment worn by a small child when his mother feels chilly

* * *

Thief: a person who finds things before the owner loses them

* * *

Trapeze artist: a guy who gets the hang of things

* * *

Tricycle: a tot rod

* * *

Twins: infant replay

* * *

Ventriloquist: a person who talks to himself for a living

* * *

Walkie-talkie: the opposite of sittie-stillie

✳ ✳ ✳

Zinc: what happens to you if you don't know how to zwim

Looney Riddles

Q: If you were drowning and had only a quarter, what would you buy?

A: A pack of lifesavers.

* * *

Q: What kind of song do you sing in a car?

A: A cartoon.

* * *

Q: What did Paul Revere say when he finished his famous ride?

A: Whoa.

* * *

Q: What did the sea say to the shore?

A: Nothing. It just waved.

* * *

Q: If you were locked in a room that had nothing in it but a calendar and a bed, what would you do for food?

A: Get water from the springs and dates from the calendar.

* * *

Q: If your dog was eating your book, what would you do?

A: I would take the words right out of his mouth.

* * *

Q: Which president had the largest family?

A: George Washington. He became the father of our country.

* * *

Q: What question can never be answered by saying yes?

A: "Are you asleep?"

* * *

Q: What kind of waiter never accepts tips?

A: A dumbwaiter.

* * *

Q: What has four legs and only one foot?

A: A bed.

* * *

Q: What should you do if someone splits their sides with laughter?

A: Have them run as fast as they can till they get a stitch in their side.

* * *

Q: What's the greatest surgical operation on record?

A: Lancing Michigan.

* * *

Q: Which is heavier, a half-moon or a full moon?

A: A half-moon, because the full moon is lighter.

* * *

Q: What do liars do after death?

A: Lie still.

* * *

Q: What is the difference between an engineer and a teacher?

A: One minds the train, and the other trains the mind.

* * *

Q: What key is the hardest to turn?

A: A donkey.

* * *

Q: What makes more noise than a cat howling at midnight?

A: Two cats howling at midnight.

* * *

Q: What kind of people go to heaven?

A: Dead ones.

* * *

Q: What has a tongue but cannot speak?

A: A shoe.

* * *

Q: What goes up but never comes down?

A: Your age.

* * *

Q: What is stranger than a talking dog?

A: A spelling bee.

* * *

Q: What makes a baseball stadium cool?

A: The fans.

* * *

Q: What does everybody give and not like to take?

A: Advice.

* * *

Q: What position on baseball teams do fishermen usually play?

A: Catcher.

* * *

Q: What kind of sentence would you get if you broke the law of gravity?

A: A suspended one.

* * *

Q: What goes uphill and downhill but always stays in the same place?

A: A road.

* * *

Q: What did the man say when he lost the fencing match?

A: Foiled again.

* * *

Q: What falls often but never gets hurt?

A: Rain.

* * *

Q: What pen is never used for writing?

A: A pig pen.

* * *

Q: What grows larger the more you take away?

A: A hole.

* * *

Q: Which vice president wore the largest hat?

A: The one with the largest head.

* * *

Q: What was the largest island before Australia was discovered?

A: Australia.

* * *

Q: What is always behind time?

A: The back of the watch.

* * *

Q: Which is larger, Mr. Larger or Mr. Larger's baby?

A: The baby is a little Larger.

* * *

Q: What day is the strongest day of the week?

A: Sunday. The rest are weak days.

* * *

Q: Which is the largest room in the world?

A: The room for improvement.

* * *

Q: What does even the cleverest person always overlook?

A: His nose.

* * *

Q: What speaks every language?

A: An echo.

* * *

Q: What does everyone desire and yet want to get rid of as soon as they get it?

A: A good appetite.

* * *

Q: What kind of tree is the oldest?

A: The elder.

* * *

Q: What is the best color for cheerleader's uniforms?

A: Yell-ow.

* * *

Q: What were Sir Isaac Newton's first words when he discovered gravity?

A: Ouch!

***

Q: What geometry symbol is like a runaway parrot?

A: A polygon.

***

Q: What is always spelled wrong?

A: "Wrong."

***

Q: What Spanish food is named after feet?

A: Burri-toes.

***

Q: What is unusual about Dutch footwear?

A: Wooden shoe like to know!

***

Q: Why don't women become bald as soon as men?

A: Because they wear their hair longer.

***

Q: What tool can cut through arctic ice?

A: A sea saw.

* * *

Q: What color is a guitar?

A: Plink!

* * *

Q: What does a real estate salesperson have to know?

A: Lots.

* * *

Q: What kind of beans do not grow in a garden?

A: Jelly beans.

* * *

Q: What has a head but can't think?

A: A match.

* * *

Q: What does the vegetable garden say when you tell it a joke?

A: Hoe, hoe, hoe!

* * *

Q: What would you call Batman and Robin if they were run over by a truck?

A: Flatman and Ribbon.

* * *

Q: What letter is never found in the alphabet?

A: The one you mail.

* * *

Q: What has 18 legs and catches flies?

A: A baseball team.

* * *

Q: What country is useful at mealtime?

A: China.

* * *

Q: What state serves as a source of metal?

A: Ore.

* * *

Q: What happens when you tickle a mule?

A: You get a big kick out of it.

* * *

Q: What do you say to a tailor about his clothes?

A: Suit yourself.

✳ ✳ ✳

Q: What did they do to the girl who stole some eye makeup?

A: She got 50 lashes.

✳ ✳ ✳

Q: What happened when a camper swallowed a flashlight?

A: He hiccupped with delight.

✳ ✳ ✳

Q: What did the wise old canary say to the parrot?

A: Talk is cheep, cheep, cheep.

✳ ✳ ✳

Q: What do bank robbers like to eat with their soup?

A: Safe crackers.

✳ ✳ ✳

Q: What question do you always have to answer by saying yes?

A: "What does y-e-s spell?"

✳ ✳ ✳

Q: If you wanted to take a bath without water, what would you do?

A: Sunbathe.

* * *

Q: What happens to a person who lies down in front of a car?

A: He gets tired.

* * *

Q: What would you say if you were invited to dinner and found nothing on the table but a beet?

A: Well, that beet's all!

* * *

Q: What's made of yellow plastic and holds up banks?

A: A robber duckie.

* * *

Q: What lives at the bottom of the sea, is brightly colored, and is popular around Easter?

A: An oyster egg.

* * *

Q: What do you call it when a violin player runs away?

A: Fiddler on the hoof.

* * *

Q: What is a liar's favorite month?

A: Fibruary.

* * *

Q: What was Dr. Jekyll's favorite game?

A: Hyde and seek.

* * *

Q: What do you do if there's a kidnapping in Texas?

A: Wake him up.

* * *

Q: What city wanders around aimlessly?

A: Rome.

* * *

Q: What is a good way to kill time in the winter?

A: Sleigh it.

* * *

Q: What is big enough to hold a pig and small enough to hold in your hands?

A: A pen.

* * *

Q: What is the best name for the wife of a lawyer?

A: Sue.

* * *

Q: What is the best name for the wife of a civil engineer?

A: Bridget.

* * *

Q: What is the difference between progress and Congress?

A: Pro and con.

* * *

Q: What kind of workers are best for hotels?

A: The inn experienced.

* * *

Q: What is appropriate material for a dairyman to wear?

A: Cheesecloth.

* * *

Q: What did one arithmetic book say to the other?

A: I've got problems.

* * *

Q: What do you call a boomerang that doesn't come back?

A: A stick.

* * *

Q: What beverage is appropriate for a golfer?

A: Tea.

* * *

Q: What is nothing but holes tied to holes yet is as strong as steel?

A: A chain.

* * *

Q: What did the bull say to the cow?

A: When I fall in love, it will be for heifer.

* * *

Q: What would you get if you crossed a radio-show host with a cheese?

A: Rush Limburger.

* * *

Q: What's red and white and blue all over?

A: A candy cane holding its breath.

* * *

Q: If you stood with your back to the north and faced due south, what would be on your left hand?

A: Fingers.

* * *

Q: Which city eats the most peaches?

A: Pits-burgh.

* * *

Q: Which city has the most canoes?

A: Oarlando.

* * *

Q: What snacks do space travelers like to eat?

A: Astronuts.

* * *

Q: What do you use to paint a picture of the ocean?

A: Watercolors.

Elephants Arise

Q: How do you know when an elephant is in your bed?

A: He has an E on his pajamas.

***

Q: How do you know when there's an elephant in your chocolate pudding?

A: When it's lumpier than usual.

***

Q: Why do elephants have flat feet?

A: From jumping out of trees.

***

Q: How does an elephant get in a tree?

A: He hides in an acorn and waits for a squirrel to carry him up.

***

Q: How did an elephant get stuck in a tree?

A: His parachute got caught.

***

Q: Why is it dangerous to go into the jungle between two and four in the afternoon?

A: Because that's when elephants are jumping out of trees.

* * *

Q: Why are pygmies so small?

A: They went into the jungle between two and four in the afternoon.

* * *

Q: What did the zookeeper say when he saw three elephants wearing sunglasses?

A: Nothing. He didn't recognize them.

* * *

Q: What would you call an elephant living in a teepee?

A: An Indian elephant.

* * *

Q: What's gray, carries flowers and candy, and visits sick people?

A: A get wellephant.

* * *

Q: What was written on the back of an elephant's pants?

A: Caution—wide load ahead.

* * *

Q: What is gray, has big ears, and is 16 feet tall?

A: An elephant on stilts.

* * *

Q: What is blue, has big ears, bulging eyes, and weighs 2,000 pounds?

A: An elephant holding its breath.

* * *

Q: How do you can an elephant?

A: You just look at him and say, "You're fired."

* * *

Q: If cowboys can tame wild horses, why don't they tame elephants?

A: Would you want to ride a bucking elephant?

* * *

Q: Why don't Eskimos keep elephants as pets?

A: Because they have a hard time squeezing them into their igloos.

* * *

Q: Where is the best place to watch an elephant pole vault?

A: A long way from the landing pit.

* * *

Q: Why did the elephant quit the circus?

A: He was tired of working for peanuts.

* * *

Q: What time is it when an elephant sits on your fence?

A: Time to buy a new fence.

* * *

Q: Why can't an elephant ride a bicycle?

A: Because it has no thumb to ring the bell.

* * *

Q: What is gray, weighs 2,000 pounds, and has four wheels?

A: An elephant on a skateboard.

* * *

Q: What did the peanut vendor say to the elephant?

A: Keep your nose out of my business.

* * *

Q: What do they call a man who herds elephants?

A: A trunk driver.

* * *

Q: How can you tell if an elephant has been in your refrigerator?

A: You can see his footprints in the butter.

* * *

Q: How do you make an elephant fly?

A: Well, first you take a really big zipper…

* * *

Q: Can elephants fly?

A: Yes. But only if they first get a pilot's license.

* * *

Q: Why do elephants have trunks?

A: Because they would look ridiculous with suitcases on their faces.

* * *

Q: Why were elephants late in getting aboard Noah's ark?

A: Because they took too long packing their trunks.

* * *

Q: Why do elephants have unlimited credit?

A: No one is brave enough to stop them from charging.

* * *

Q: Why was the girl elephant late for her first date?

A: Because she took too long to powder her nose.

* * *

Q: Why are elephants so smart?

A: Because they have tons of gray matter.

* * *

Q: What's as big as an elephant, looks like an elephant, but doesn't weigh an ounce?

A: An elephant's shadow.

* * *

Q: What has a trunk, weighs 2,000 pounds, and is red all over?

A: An elephant with a very bad sunburn.

* * *

Q: Why did the small elephant spend two hours in the bathtub?

A: Because his mother ordered him to wash behind his ears.

* * *

Q: How do you fit six elephants in a motorboat?

A: Put three in the front seat and three in the back seat.

✳ ✳ ✳

Q: What's the difference between a chocolate chip cookie and an elephant?

A: You can't dunk an elephant in your milk.

✳ ✳ ✳

Q: Why do elephants never get rich?

A: Because they work for peanuts.

✳ ✳ ✳

Q: What's the difference between a mouse and an elephant?

A: About 2,000 pounds.

✳ ✳ ✳

Q: What is the biggest ant in the world?

A: An eleph-ant.

✳ ✳ ✳

Q: What's gray, weighs 2,000 pounds, and spins around like a top?

A: An elephant stuck in a revolving door.

✳ ✳ ✳

First boy: Why do elephants paint themselves orange?

Second boy: I don't know.

First boy: So they can hide in orange trees.

Second boy: I've never seen an elephant in an orange tree.

First boy: That's because they do such a good job of hiding.

* * *

Boy: What's the difference between an elephant and a matterbaby?

Girl: What's a matterbaby?

Boy: Nothing. I didn't know you cared.

* * *

First trainer: Why is the ground shaking?

Second trainer: Oh, that's nothing. It's just the elephants playing leapfrog.

Why Do They Do That?

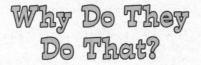

Q: Why did the chicken cross the road?

A: For foul reasons.

* * *

Q: Why did the three little pigs decide to leave home?

A: They thought their father was an awful boar.

* * *

Q: Why does a hen lay an egg?

A: Because she can't lay a brick.

* * *

Q: Why do rabbits get up early in the morning when the ground is wet?

A: So they can get a hare dew.

* * *

Q: Why did the skunk go to the hospital?

A: He was feeling out of odor.

* * *

Q: Why was the rabbit being punished?

A: Because he was having a bad hare day.

* * *

Q: Why did the baby deer wave at the grown-up deer?

A: Because he was passing the buck.

* * *

Q: Why was the lion so arrogant?

A: Because he had a large pride.

* * *

Q: Why was the big cat disqualified from a race?

A: Because he was a cheetah.

* * *

Q: Why are hyenas awful storytellers?

A: Because they have no tales to speak of.

* * *

Q: Why did the zoo animals think the giraffe was conceited?

A: Because its nose was always up in the air.

* * *

Q: Why was the mouse crying?

A: Because he was peeling an onion.

* * *

Q: Why did the buck kiss the deer?

A: Because they were standing under the mistle-doe.

* * *

Q: Why did the fish go to the doctor?

A: It wasn't feeling whale.

* * *

Q: Why did the chicken cross the playground?

A: To get to the other slide.

* * *

Q: Why did the pony go to the school nurse?

A: It was a little horse.

* * *

Q: Why did the runaway thief hate dogs?

A: They kept hounding him.

* * *

Q: Why was the big animal always afraid he was sick?

A: He was a hippochondriac.

* * *

Q: Why are spiders like tops?

A: They are always spinning.

* * *

Q: Why are sheep poor?

A: Because they're always getting fleeced.

* * *

Q: Why are fish smart?

A: Because they swim in schools.

* * *

Q: Why is it so hard to fool a snake?

A: You can't pull his leg.

* * *

Q: Why did the lion build a fence?

A: He wanted a prey pen.

* * *

Q: Why is it hard to talk with a goat around?

A: Because he always butts in.

* * *

Q: Why was the pig thrown out of the soccer match?

A: He played dirty.

* * *

Q: Why was the cat given an award at the end of the year?

A: It had purrrrrrfect attendance.

* * *

Q: Why did the spider get an A in the computer class?

A: Because it was good at surfing the web.

* * *

Q: Why wasn't the rowdy pig invited to the party?

A: He was known for going hog wild.

* * *

Q: Why wasn't the quiet pig invited to the party?

A: He was boaring.

* * *

Q: Why do rabbits always look so cute?

A: They use hare brushes and hare spray.

12

Colorful Characters

Q: What's black and white and red all over?

A: A sloppy zebra eating tomato soup.

* * *

Q: What's black and white and lumpy?

A: A zebra with mumps.

* * *

Q: What's black and white and blue?

A: A zebra with a sad story.

* * *

Q: What's black and white and green all over?

A: A zebra rolling in the lettuce.

* * *

Q: What's black and white with splashes of red?

A: A zebra and a penguin in a rotten tomato fight.

* * *

Q: What's black and white and green?

A: A zebra with lettuce in his teeth.

* * *

Q: What's red and red and red all over?

A: Measles with a sunburn.

* * *

Q: What's big and white and lives in the Sahara Desert?

A: A lost polar bear.

13

What's What?

Q: What's the value of the moon?

A: Four quarters.

＊＊＊

Q: What's worse than raining cats and dogs?

A: Hailing taxis and buses.

＊＊＊

Q: What's too much for one, enough for two, but nothing at all for three?

A: A secret.

＊＊＊

Q: What's the best key to a good dinner?

A: A turkey.

＊＊＊

Q: What's the difference between a hill and a pill?

A: One is hard to get up and the other is hard to get down.

＊＊＊

Q: What's the best way to raise strawberries?

A: With a spoon.

* * *

Q: What's the difference between a rain cloud and a whipped child?

A: One pours with rain, and the other roars with pain.

* * *

Q: What's full of holes and yet holds water?

A: A sponge.

* * *

Q: What's so brittle that it can be broken just by naming it?

A: Silence.

* * *

Q: What is easy to get into but hard to get out of?

A: Trouble.

* * *

Q: What is the difference between a boxing champion and a man with a cold?

A: One knows his blows and the other blows his nose.

14

From A to Z

Q: Who is the smartest pupil in the alphabet?

A: The A student.

* * *

Q: Why is E the most unfortunate of all the letters?

A: Because it is never in cash, always in debt, and never out of danger.

* * *

Q: Why is the letter E like London?

A: Because it is the capital in England.

* * *

Q: What is at the end of everything?

A: The letter G.

* * *

Q: What letter is a part of the head?

A: I.

* * *

Q: Who is the saddest letter in the alphabet?

A: The blue J.

* * *

Q: What letter is a vegetable?

A: P.

* * *

Q: How do you make the number seven, even?

A: Take away the S.

* * *

Q: What's the difference between here and there?

A: The letter T.

* * *

Q: What's the center of gravity?

A: The letter V.

* * *

Q: What changes a lad into a lady?

A: The letter Y.

* * *

Q: What letter is nine inches long?

A: The letter Y—it's one-fourth of a yard.

15

When, Then?

Q: When does a boat show affection?

A: When it hugs the shore.

* * *

Q: When is a piece of wood like a queen?

A: When it is made into a ruler.

* * *

Q: When does a leopard change his spots?

A: When he moves.

* * *

Q: When are cooks most cruel?

A: When they beat the eggs and whip the cream.

* * *

Q: When was beef the highest it has ever been?

A: When the cow jumped over the moon.

* * *

Q: When does a mouse weigh as much as an elephant?

A: When the scale is broken.

* * *

Q: When does a teacher wear dark glasses?

A: When she has bright pupils.

* * *

Q: When does it rain money?

A: Whenever there's change in the weather.

* * *

Q: When is a rope like a piece of wood?

A: When it has knots.

* * *

Q: When is a gardener like a story writer?

A: When he works up his plot.

* * *

Q: When is a pint of milk not a pint?

A: When it's condensed.

* * *

Q: When is a cigar like dried beef?

A: When it is smoked.

***

Q: When is an airplane not an airplane?

A: When it's aloft.

***

Q: When do you have four hands?

A: When you double your fists.

***

Q: When is a boy not a boy?

A: When he's a little hoarse.

***

Q: When is a blow on the head like a piece of fabric?

A: When it is felt.

***

Q: When is a sailor not a sailor?

A: When he's aboard.

***

Q: When does a public speaker steal lumber?

A: When he takes the floor.

* * *

Q: When can a giant be small?

A: When he's with his big brother.

* * *

Q: When is a store like a boat?

A: When it has sales.

* * *

Q: When can a man be tall and short at the same time?

A: When he's six feet six but short of money.

* * *

Q: When is it a good thing to lose your temper?

A: When it is a bad one.

* * *

Q: When is a black dog not a black dog?

A: When he is a greyhound.

* * *

Q: When its cold outside, what country are you in?

A: Chile.

* * *

Q: When a librarian goes fishing, what does she use for bait?

A: Bookworms.

* * *

Q: When the clock strikes 13, what time is it?

A: Time to get the clock fixed.

* * *

Q: When is a computer dangerous?

A: When it crashes.

Who Knew?

Q: Who makes shoes without using any leather or rubber?

A: A blacksmith.

∗∗∗

Q: Who was the biggest bandit in history?

A: Atlas. He held up the world.

∗∗∗

Q: Who brings the monster's babies?

A: Frankenstork.

∗∗∗

Q: Who carries a big sack and bites people?

A: Santa Jaws.

∗∗∗

Q: Who is Santa Claus's wife?

A: Mary Christmas.

∗∗∗

Q: Who dares to sit before the queen with his hat on?

A: Her chauffeur.

***

Q: Who makes up jokes about knitting?

A: A knitwit.

***

Q: Who is the smallest man in history?

A: The sailor who went to sleep on his watch.

17

How, Now?

Q: How do you know that peanuts are fattening?
A: Have you ever seen a skinny elephant?

* * *

Q: How do you go on a Chinese diet?
A: Use one chopstick.

* * *

Q: How did the chimpanzee get out of his cage?
A: He used a monkey wrench.

* * *

Q: How many insects does it take to make a landlord?
A: Ten ants.

* * *

Q: How does a hot coffee pot feel?
A: Perky.

* * *

Q: How did the man describe his work in the towel factory?

A: Very absorbing.

* * *

Q: How many skunks does it take to smell up the neighborhood?

A: Just a phew.

* * *

Q: How did the wood shaving fly from the board?

A: It took off on a plane.

* * *

Q: How do you make an apple turnover?

A: Tickle it in the ribs.

* * *

Q: How can you find a lost rabbit?

A: Make a noise like a carrot.

* * *

Q: How can you double your money quick?

A: Fold it over and put it into your pocket.

* * *

Q: How does an egg get to work?

A: It drives a yolkswagon.

* * *

Q: How do you find a missing barber?

A: Comb the city.

* * *

Q: How do you put out a fire at the post office?

A: Stamp it out.

* * *

Q: How do you count a herd of cows?

A: With a cowculator.

* * *

Q: How did they know the invisible man had no children?

A: Because he wasn't apparent.

* * *

Q: How do bears walk around?

A: With bear feet.

* * *

Q: How does the man in the moon cut his hair?

A: Eclipse it.

* * *

Q: How does a mouse feel after it takes a bath?

A: Squeaky clean.

* * *

Q: How can you jump off a 50-foot ladder and not get hurt?

A: Jump off the first step.

* * *

Q: How do you lock a cemetery?

A: With a skeleton key.

* * *

Q: How does one dinosaur tell another dinosaur to hurry?

A: "Pronto, Saurus!"

* * *

Q: How many balls of string would it take to reach the moon?

A: One, if it were long enough.

* * *

Q: How can five people divide five pieces of cake so that each gets a piece, and yet one piece remains on the plate?

A: The last person takes the plate with one piece of cake on it.

***

Q: How is a wig like a lie?

A: It's a false hood.

***

Q: How are worries like babies?

A: The more you nurse them, the larger they grow.

***

Q: How do you get rid of a Dalmatian?

A: Use spot remover.

***

Q: How do locomotives hear?

A: Through their engine ears.

***

Q: How do you get water into watermelons?

A: You plant them in the spring.

***

Q: How do you keep a dog from barking in the back of the car?

A: Put him in the front seat.

* * *

Q: How many controls do you have on your TV set?

A: Six, most of the time—my father, my mother, and my four sisters.

* * *

Q: How can you put yourself through a keyhole?

A: Write "yourself" on a piece of paper and push it through.

* * *

Q: How can you carry water in a sieve?

A: Freeze it first.

* * *

Q: How do you make a strawberry shake?

A: Take it to a horror film.

* * *

Q: How do you stop a gelatin race?

A: Shout, "Get set!"

* * *

Q: How did the man feel when he got his electric bill?

A: He was shocked.

* * *

Q: How do you know that eating carrots is good for the eyes?

A: Have you ever seen a rabbit wearing eyeglasses?

* * *

Q: How are talkative people like male pigs?

A: After a while, they become bores.

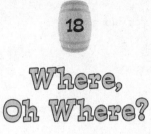

Where, Oh Where?

Q: Where was the Declaration of Independence signed?

A: At the bottom.

* * *

Q: Where did the rooster crow so loudly that all the world could hear him?

A: In Noah's Ark.

* * *

Q: Where can you always find happiness?

A: In the dictionary.

* * *

Q: Where are the largest diamonds in New York City kept?

A: In baseball stadiums.

* * *

Q: Where do sick ships go?

A: To the docs.

* * *

Q: Where does a chimney sweep keep his brushes?

A: In a soot case.

* * *

Q: Where can you see man eating plants?

A: In a vegetarian restaurant.

* * *

Q: Where did Julius Caesar go on his thirty-ninth birthday?

A: Into his fortieth year.

* * *

Q: Where does a golfer dance?

A: At the golf ball.

* * *

Q: Where does a fencing instructor go at noon?

A: Out to lunge.

* * *

Q: Where does a snowflake dance?

A: At the snowball.

* * *

Q: Where did the king's son go to college?

A: Princeton.

19

Why in the World...?

Q: Why didn't the pilot pass his flying class?

A: His grades weren't high enough.

✳✳✳

Q: Why can't it rain for two days continually?

A: Because there is always a night in between.

✳✳✳

Q: Why is an empty matchbox superior to any other?

A: It's matchless.

✳✳✳

Q: Why is a pair of skates like a forbidden fruit in the Garden of Eden?

A: Because they both have to do with the fall of man.

✳✳✳

Q: Why are adding machines so reliable?

A: Because you can count on them.

✳✳✳

Q: Why do we all go to bed?

A: Because the bed can't come to us.

* * *

Q: Why does a fireman wear red suspenders?

A: To hold up his pants.

* * *

Q: Why did the jellyroll?

A: Because it saw the apple turnover.

* * *

Q: Why did the boy buy a canary instead of a parrot?

A: It was cheeper.

* * *

Q: Why did the little girl eat bullets?

A: Because she wanted to grow bangs.

* * *

Q: Why do eggs go to the gym?

A: They like to eggsercise.

* * *

Q: Why did the jailed man want to catch the measles?

A: So he could break out.

***

Q: Why is your sense of touch impaired when you are ill?

A: Because you don't feel well.

***

Q: Why are country people smarter than city people?

A: The population is denser in big cities.

***

Q: Why can't you keep secrets in a bank?

A: Because of all the tellers.

***

Q: Why did the little boy take an umbrella to church?

A: Because he heard the pastor was going to preach up a storm.

***

Q: Why should the number 288 never be mentioned in polite company?

A: It's two gross.

***

Q: Why do they name the tree dogwood?

A: Because of its bark.

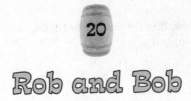

Rob and Bob

Rob: Were you able to install a new muffler in your car?

Bob: Yes, but it was exhausting.

* * *

Rob: I think my wife is getting tired of me.

Bob: What makes you feel that way?

Rob: She keeps wrapping my lunches in road maps.

* * *

Rob: I shot my dog.

Bob: Was he mad?

Rob: Well, it didn't seem to exactly please him.

* * *

Rob: What sign were you born under?

Bob: "Quiet—Hospital Zone."

* * *

Rob: Did you hear the smartest kid in the world is becoming deaf?

Bob: No, tell me about it.

Rob: What did you say?

* * *

Rob: Does the Bible say that if you smoke, you can't get to heaven?

Bob: No, but the more you smoke, the quicker you'll get there.

* * *

Rob: Be quiet, please. You're interrupting my train of thought.

Bob: Let me know when it comes to a station.

* * *

Husband: I know you are having a lot of trouble with the baby, dear, but keep in mind, "the hand that rocks the cradle rules the world."

Wife: How about taking over the world for a few hours while I go shopping?

* * *

Husband: I slept like a log.

Wife: Yes, I heard the sawmill.

* * *

Woman: One of your bees just stung me. I want you to do something about it.

Beekeeper: Certainly, ma'am. Just show me which bee it was, and I'll have it punished.

* * *

Beverly: A scientist says that we become what we eat.

Melba: Oh, boy! Let's order something rich.

* * *

Mother: Did you push your little sister down the stairs?

Bobby: I only pushed her down one step. She fell the rest of the way.

Bible Fun

Q: What are two of the smallest insects mentioned in the Bible?

A: The widow's mites and the wicked flee (Mark 12:42; Proverbs 28:1).

* * *

Q: After Cain left the Garden of Eden, he took a nap. How do we know this?

A: Because he went to the land of Nod (Genesis 4:16).

* * *

Q: Where is the first math problem mentioned in the Bible?

A: When God divided the light from the darkness (Genesis 1:4).

* * *

Q: Where is the second math problem mentioned in the Bible?

A: When God told Adam and Eve to go forth and multiply (Genesis 1:28).

* * *

Q: Who was the first person in the Bible to eat herself out of house and home?

A: Eve.

* * *

Q: Who was the straightest man in the Bible?

A: Joseph. Pharaoh made a ruler out of him.

* * *

Q: Who introduced the first walking stick?

A: Eve…when she presented Adam with a little Cain.

* * *

Q: Why was Moses the most wicked man in the Bible?

A: Because he broke the Ten Commandments all at once.

* * *

Q: Was there any money on Noah's ark?

A: Yes. The duck had a bill, the frog had a greenback, and the skunk had a scent.

* * *

Q: Who was the best financier in the Bible?

A: Noah. He floated his stock while the whole world was in liquidation.

* * *

Q: Where does the Bible talk about Hondas?

A: In Acts 1:14: "These all continued with one accord."

* * *

Q: What city in the Bible was named after something that you find on every car?

A: Tyre.

* * *

Q: When the ark landed on Mount Ararat, was Noah the first one out?

A: No, the Bible says he came forth.

* * *

Q: Which one of Noah's sons was considered a clown?

A: Ham.

* * *

Q: Where was deviled ham mentioned in the Bible?

A: When the evil spirits entered the swine.

* * *

Q: What man in the Bible spoke when he was a very small baby?

A: Job. He cursed the day he was born.

To learn more about Harvest House books and
to read sample chapters, visit our website:

www.harvesthousepublishers.com

HARVEST HOUSE PUBLISHERS
EUGENE, OREGON